Great Bustard

The World's Heaviest Flying Bird

by Kirsten Hall

Consultants: David and Karen Waters
Founders of The Great Bustard Group

BEARPORT
PUBLISHING

New York, New York

Credits

Cover, ©Carlos Sanchez/OSF/Animals Animals-Earth Scenes; 2–3, ©Roger Tidman/NHPA; 4, Kathryn Ayer; 4–5, ©Jorge Sierra/VIREO; 6, ©Brian Coster/NHPA; 7BKG, ©Bill Coster/NHPA; 8 (inset), ©Jean François Noblet/BIOS/Peter Arnold; 8–9, ©Jorge Sierra/VIREO; 10, ©DavidTipling.com; 11, ©Jorge Sierra/VIREO; 12, ©DavidTipling.com; 13, ©Brian Coster/NHPA; 14, ©Roger Tidman/NHPA; 15, ©Carlos Sanchez Alonso/Oxford Scientific; 16 (inset), ©Frank Lane Picture Agency/Corbis; 16–17, ©Derrick England; 18–19, ©Jorge Sierra/VIREO; 20, ©Bert Wikund; 21, ©M. Watson/Ardea.com; 22L, ©Mike Lane/WWI/Peter Arnold; 22C, ©John Cancalosi/Peter Arnold; 22R, ©Frederic Pawlowski/Peter Arnold; 23TL, ©Derrick England; 23TR, ©Carlos Sanchez Alonso/Oxford Scientific; 23BL, ©Brian Coster/NHPA; 23BR, ©John MacGregor/Peter Arnold; 23BKG, ©Hellio & Van Ingen/NHPA.

Publisher: Kenn Goin
Editorial Director: Adam Siegel
Editorial Development: Nancy Hall, Inc.
Creative Director: Spencer Brinker
Photo Researcher: Carousel Research, Inc.: Mary Teresa Giancoli
Design: Otto Carbajal

Library of Congress Cataloging-in-Publication Data

Hall, Kirsten.
 Great bustard : the world's heaviest flying bird / by Kirsten Hall ; consultants, David and Karen Waters of the Great Bustard Group.
    p. cm.—(SuperSized!)
 Includes bibliographical references and index.
 ISBN-13: 978-1-59716-390-3 (library binding)
 ISBN-10: 1-59716-390-2 (library binding)
 1. Great bustard—Juvenile literature. I. Title.

 QL696.G86H35 2007
 598.3'2—dc22

                    2006032751

For more information, write to Bearport Publishing Company, Inc., 101 Fifth Avenue, Suite 6R, New York, New York 10003. Printed in the United States of America.

10 9 8 7 6 5 4 3 2 1

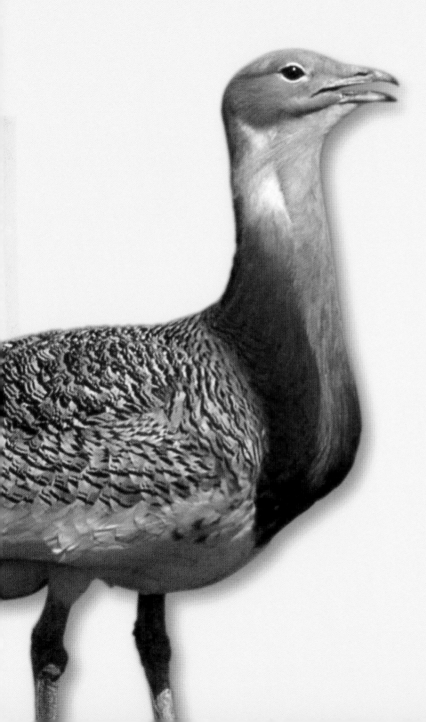

Contents

A Heavy Flyer

The great bustard is the heaviest flying bird in the world.

A male great bustard weighs about the same as a bulldog.

A male great bustard can weigh up to 46 pounds (21 kg). A female great bustard can weigh up to 11 pounds (5 kg).

Grassy Homes

Great bustards live on **grasslands** in Europe, Asia, and Africa.

They are also found on large farms there.

Male bustards gather in **droves**. The groups start out with a few birds. More join until the droves have up to several hundred birds.

Great Bustards in the Wild

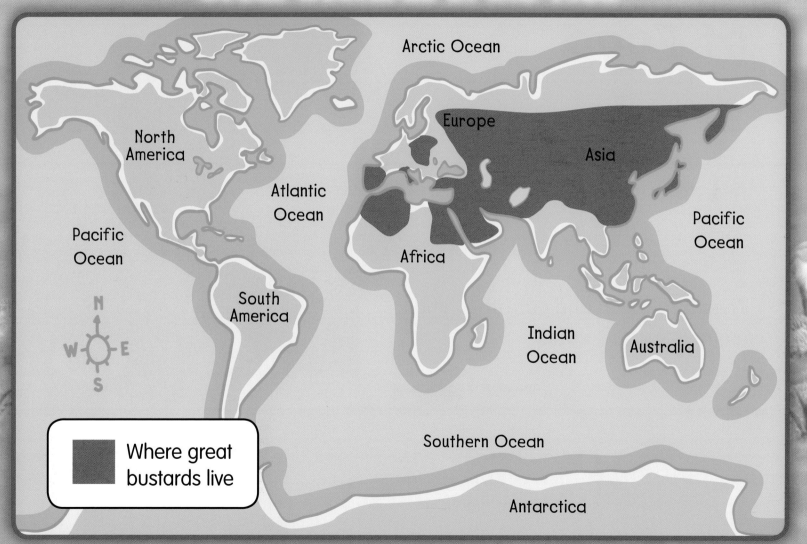

Arctic Ocean

North America

Europe

Asia

Atlantic Ocean

Pacific Ocean

Pacific Ocean

Africa

South America

Indian Ocean

Australia

N
W   E
S

Where great bustards live

Southern Ocean

Antarctica

All Kinds of Food

Great bustards eat mostly plants.

Kale and cabbage are two of their favorites.

Sometimes the birds hunt insects, spiders, and frogs.

They also catch and eat other small animals such as **voles**.

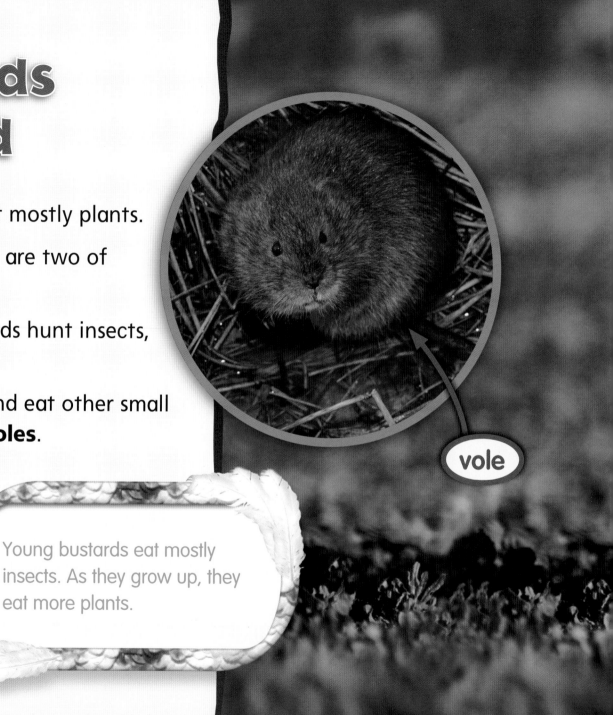

vole

Young bustards eat mostly insects. As they grow up, they eat more plants.

8

Big Wings

The great bustard has big, strong wings.

While flying, this heavy bird must flap its wings at all times.

Lighter birds can flap their wings and then glide.

If a great bustard tried to glide, it would fall to the ground.

A male great bustard's wings are about 7 feet (2.1 m) long from tip to tip.

Hiding from Enemies

Foxes are the great bustard's main enemy.

Bustards hide from them behind tall plants.

If a fox sees them, these big birds run or fly away.

A great bustard can run faster than a fox.

Putting on a Show

In spring, male bustards puff out their neck feathers.

They dance in front of female bustards.

They try to get the females to notice them.

After the dance, the females choose which males they will have babies with.

female bustard

Great bustards are silent most of the time. Males sometimes bark at other males when they fight.

male
bustard

Baby Bustards

A great bustard mother scrapes out a small hole in the ground as her nest.

She lays two or three eggs.

After a few weeks, the **chicks** hatch from the eggs.

When chicks hatch they are about as long as a new crayon. They weigh about as much as an apple.

great bustard egg

Fast Learners

Great bustard chicks can walk soon after they hatch.

At two months, they start trying to fly.

They stretch and flap their wings while running.

By three months, the chicks are flying!

Great bustard chicks stay close to their mother until they are about one year old.

Helping the Great Bustard

Great bustards are in danger.

People build on the farms where they live.

Hunters kill bustards for food.

Today, people are working to protect these big, flying birds.

A great bustard lives about 10 to 15 years.

More Heavy Birds

Great bustards are a kind of bird. All birds are warm-blooded, have feathers, and lay eggs. Most birds fly. A few, such as the ostrich and the penguin, cannot.

Here are three more heavy birds that fly.

Mute Swan

The mute swan is a heavy waterbird. A mute swan can weigh up to 27 pounds (12 kg).

California Condor

The California condor can weigh up to 23 pounds (10.4 kg).

Albatross

The albatross can weigh up to 22 pounds (10 kg).

Great Bustard: 46 pounds/21 kg

Mute Swan: 27 pounds/12 kg

California Condor: 23 pounds/10.4 kg

Albatross: 22 pounds/10 kg

Glossary

chicks (CHIKS) birds that are very young

grasslands (GRASS-landz) large, open areas of land where grass grows

droves (DROHVZ) large groups of animals moving together

voles (VOHLZ) small, furry animals that look like mice

Index

Read More

Copeland, Cynthia L., and Alexandra P. Lewis. *Funny Faces, Wacky Wings, and Other Silly Big Bird Things.* Brookfield, CT: Millbrook Press (2002).

Tesar, Jenny. *What on Earth Is a Bustard?* Woodbridge, CT: Blackbirch Press (1996).

Learn More Online

To learn more about great bustards, visit **www.bearportpublishing.com/SuperSized**